FOLK COSTUMES OF EUROPE
Coloring Book

Rendered for Coloring by
Susan Johnston

Dover Publications, Inc., New York

Introduction

Because of its simple but graceful forms and its delight in the use of bright colors, folk art has always been one of the world's most popular art forms. Although perhaps less widely known and appreciated than folk painting, ceramics and music, the subject of this book—folk costume—is a very important part of this general topic. It is, in fact, a particularly fascinating aspect because it is not *one* art but several, combining many different traditional handicrafts, such as embroidery, appliqué, beadwork, weaving and patchwork. And just as folk design has always been a source of inspiration to professional artists, so has folk costume constantly renewed and enlivened the world of fashion design. Even today, for example, the "peasant look" is once again creating a great stir.

For this book Susan Johnston has rendered over 130 folk costumes from many different areas of Europe. They are based on accurate and detailed illustrations that were originally published in a famous German magazine, the *Mün-chener Bilderbogen,* in the late 19th century.* At that time European peasants still wore these traditional costumes frequently, but since then these elaborate clothes have become rarer and rarer and are now to be seen only on special festive occasions and in museums.

As the captions point out, some of the locales mentioned have been known by different names. For example, the Italian city of Cassino (Plate 5) used to be known as San Germano, and the town of Bressanone (Plate 33) in the Alto Adige region of Italy is known to German-speaking people as Brixen.

In coloring these drawings, indulge yourself in gay color schemes, using bright reds, yellows, blues and greens. The color plates on the covers of this book provide some suggestions, but you can work out many others on your own. You will also find it interesting to adapt color schemes from folk paintings and pieces of pottery that you see in museums or in books and magazines.

---

* If you develop a real interest in folk costume, you may want to study the complete series of over 1400 costume designs from this magazine which have been reprinted by Dover Publications, Inc., under the title *Historic Costume in Pictures.*

Published in Canada by General Publishing Company, Ltd., 30 Lesmill Road, Don Mills, Toronto, Ontario.

Published in the United Kingdom by Constable and Company, Ltd., 3 The Lanchesters, 162–164 Fulham Palace Road, London W6 9ER.

Folk Costumes of Europe Coloring Book is a new work, first published by Dover Publications, Inc., in 1977. The 45 illustrations rendered for coloring by Susan Johnston are based on plates in Braun & Schneider, *Historic Costume in Pictures*, Dover Publications, Inc., 1975 (which is, in turn, an anthology of all the folk costume illustrations originally published in *Münchener Bilderbogen* between 1861 and 1890).

DOVER *Pictorial Archive* SERIES

International Standard Book Number: 0-486-23513-0

Manufactured in the United States of America
Dover Publications, Inc.
31 East 2nd Street
Mineola, N.Y. 11501

1. **SPAIN.** *Left*: couple from Alicante. *Right*: couple from Zamora.

2. **SPAIN.** *Left*: a man from León. *Right*: a group from Segovia.

3. SPAIN. A group from Murcia.

4. SPAIN. *Left*: couple from Valencia. *Right*: couple from Granada.

5. ITALY. *Left*: two men from San Germano (Cassino). *Right*: two women from the Roman coast.

6. ITALY. Group on the outskirts of Rome.

7. ITALY. *Left*: two women from Genzano, near Rome. *Right*: piper
from the Neapolitan Apennines.

8. **ITALY.** *Left and right*: two women from the Volscian (Lepini) Mountains of Italy. *Center*: fisherman from the Neapolitan Apennines.

9. THE NETHERLANDS. Man and woman from Scheveningen.

10. THE NETHERLANDS. Women from Friesland.

11. THE NETHERLANDS. *Left*: man with pipe. *Right*: woman with basket and jug.

12. THE NETHERLANDS. Family group.

13. FRANCE. Group from Brittany.

14. FRANCE. Two men from Brittany.

15. FRANCE. Young couple from Brittany.

16. FRANCE. Two women and a man from Brittany.

17. ALSACE. *Left to right*: women from the villages of Kochersberg, near
Strasbourg; Krautgersheim (Schlettstadt); Colmar; and Oberseebach.

18. ALSACE. *Left*: man from Aschbach. *Center*: woman from Weissenburg.
Right: woman from Kochersberg.

19. SWITZERLAND. *Left*: woman from Berne. *Right*: woman from Simmental.

20. SWITZERLAND. *Left*: woman from the Valais. *Right*: woman from Unterwalden.

21. **NORTH GERMANY.** *Left*: a couple from the Vierlande. *Right*: a peasant woman from Nottendorf (Geest).

22. **NORTH GERMANY.** *Left*: a woman in Communion dress from Schleswig-Holstein. *Center*: a peasant from Hohenwestedt. *Right*: a woman from the Halligen.

23. GERMANY (Baden). Wedding costumes from Hauenstein.

24. GERMANY (Baden). Group from Western Baar.

25. GERMANY (Baden). Two men and a woman from Eastern Baar.

26. GERMANY (Baden). Couple from the Hanau region.

27. GERMANY (Bavaria). Two young women from Miesbach.

28. GERMANY (Bavaria). Two men from Miesbach.

29. **GERMANY** (Bavaria). Two men from Starnberg, near Munich.

30. GERMANY (Bavaria). Two women from Starnberg.

31. **THE TYROL** (Italian Alps). Two men from Meran (Merano).

32. THE TYROL. Couple from the Grödner Valley.

33. **THE TYROL.** *Left and right*: couple from Brixen (Bressanone)
Valley. *Center*: a man from Unterwangenberg.

34. YUGOSLAVIA. *Left*: couple from Kruzevice (Crivoscie). *Right*: two
porters from Dubrovnik (Ragusa).

35. YUGOSLAVIA. *Far left and right*: man and woman from Gruda, near Dubrovnik. *Two figures at center*: man and woman from Risan, Boka Kotorska (Risano, bocche di Cattaro).

36. YUGOSLAVIA. *Left*: woman from Draste. *Right*: three women from Kruzevice, Boka Kotorska.

37. **THE BALKANS.** *Left*: man from Tartaro, near Sibenik (Sebenico).
Center: woman from the islands off Sibenik. *Right*: girl from Bukovica.

38. THE BALKANS. *Left to right*: a man from Shkodër (Scutari), Albania; a woman from Prizren, Yugoslavia; an Arnaut (Albanian) from Yanina, Greece; and a Bulgar.

39. **THE BALKANS.** *Left*: Kurdish woman from Juzgat. *Right*: two women from Préveza and Chios.

40. **THE BALKANS.** *Left*: a couple from Shkodër (Scutari), Albania.
Center: a man from Adrianople (Edirne), Turkey. *Right*: a woman
from Thessaloniki (Salonica), Greece.

41. THE BALKANS. *Left*: a couple from Monastir, Yugoslavia. *Right*: a woman from Thessaly, Greece.

42. RUSSIA. Tatars from the Crimea.

43. RUSSIA. *Left*: a Volga Finn from the Mordovian Republic. *Second from left*: a Cheremiss (Mari) woman. *Right*: two Estonians.

44. **RUSSIA.** *Left*: woman from Yaroslavl. *Center*: woman from Tver (Kalinin). *Right*: a man and woman from Kaluga.

45. **RUSSIA AND FINLAND.** *Left*: a woman from Ryazan. *Figure at back*: a man from the Guberniya of Voronezh. *Seated figure*: a Finnish woman. *Right*: a woman from the Guberniya of Petersburg.

DOVER COLORING BOOKS

FAVORITE ROSES COLORING BOOK, Ilil Arbel. (25845-9) $2.95

FUN WITH SEARCH-A-WORD COLORING BOOK, Nina Barbaresi.
(26327-4) $2.50

FUN WITH SPELLING COLORING BOOK, Nina Barbaresi. (25999-4) $2.50

JEWISH HOLIDAYS AND TRADITIONS COLORING BOOK, Chaya Burstein.
(26322-3) $2.95

INDIAN TRIBES OF NORTH AMERICA COLORING BOOK, Peter F. Copeland.
(26303-7) $2.95

BIRDS OF PREY COLORING BOOK, John Green. (25989-7) $2.95

LIFE IN ANCIENT EGYPT COLORING BOOK, John Green and Stanley
Appelbaum. (26130-1) $2.95

WHALES AND DOLPHINS COLORING BOOK, John Green. (26306-1) $2.95

DINOSAUR ABC COLORING BOOK, Llyn Hunter. (25786-X) $2.50

SHARKS OF THE WORLD COLORING BOOK, Llyn Hunter. (26137-9) $2.95

HISTORY OF SPACE EXPLORATION COLORING BOOK, Bruce LaFontaine.
(26152-2) $2.95

HOLIDAYS STAINED GLASS COLORING BOOK, Ted Menten. (26062-3) $3.95

FUN WITH OPPOSITES COLORING BOOK, Anna Pomaska and Suzanne Ross.
(25983-8) $2.50

DINOSAUR LIFE ACTIVITY BOOK, Donald Silver and Patricia Wynne.
(25809-2) $2.50

HISTORY OF THE AMERICAN AUTOMOBILE COLORING BOOK, A. G. Smith and
Randy Mason. (26315-0) $2.95

THE VELVETEEN RABBIT COLORING BOOK, Margery Williams and Thea
Kliros. (25924-2) $2.95

HEBREW ALPHABET COLORING BOOK, Chaya Burstein. (25089-X) $2.95

COLUMBUS DISCOVERS AMERICA COLORING BOOK, Peter F. Copeland.
(25542-5) $2.75

STORY OF THE AMERICAN REVOLUTION COLORING BOOK, Peter Copeland.
(25648-0) $2.95

FAVORITE POEMS FOR CHILDREN COLORING BOOK, illustrated by Susan
Gaber. (23923-3) $2.95

HORSES OF THE WORLD COLORING BOOK, John Green. (24985-9) $2.95

WILD ANIMALS COLORING BOOK, John Green. (25476-3) $2.95

THE DAYS OF THE DINOSAUR COLORING BOOK, Matthew Kalmenoff.
(25359-7) $2.95

SMALL ANIMALS OF NORTH AMERICA COLORING BOOK, Elizabeth A.
McClelland. (24217-X) $2.95

Paperbound unless otherwise indicated. Prices subject to change without notice. Available at your book dealer or write for free catalogues to Dept. 23, Dover Publications, Inc., 31 East 2nd Street, Mineola, N.Y. 11501. Please indicate field of interest. Each year Dover publishes over 200 books on fine art, music, crafts and needlework, antiques, languages, literature, children's books, chess, cookery, nature, anthropology, science, mathematics, and other areas.

Manufactured in the U.S.A.